Comhairle Contae
Átha Cliath Theas
South Dublin County Council

COUNTRY PROFILES

VIETNAM

BY EMILY ROSE OACHS

BELLWETHER MEDIA • MINNEAPOLIS, MN

Blastoff! Discovery launches
a new mission: reading to learn.
Filled with facts and features, each
book offers you an exciting new
world to explore!

This edition first published in 2018 by Bellwether Media, Inc.

No part of this publication may be reproduced in whole or in part
without written permission of the publisher.
For information regarding permission, write to Bellwether Media, Inc.,
Attention: Permissions Department,
5357 Penn Avenue South, Minneapolis, MN 55419.

Library of Congress Cataloging-in-Publication Data

Names: Oachs, Emily Rose, author.
Title: Vietnam / by Emily Rose Oachs.
Description: Minneapolis, MN : Bellwether Media, Inc., 2018. |
   Series: Blastoff! Discovery: Country Profiles | Includes bibliographical
   references and index. | Audience: Grades 3-8.
Identifiers: LCCN 2017035835 (print) | LCCN 2017036309 (ebook)
   | ISBN 9781626177376 hardcover : alk. paper) | ISBN
   9781681034911 (ebook)
Subjects: LCSH: Vietnam–Juvenile literature.
Classification: LCC DS556.3 (ebook) | LCC DS556.3 .O23 2018
   (print) | DDC 959.7–dc23
LC record available at https://lccn.loc.gov/2017035835

Editor: Paige V. Polinsky   Designer: Brittany McIntosh

Printed in the United States of America, North Mankato, MN.

TABLE OF CONTENTS

A group of hikers explores Hang Son Doong. The cave rests in the middle of Phong Nha-Ke Bang National Park. The hikers pass wide underground rivers and wander through huge caverns filled with soft mist. Dark limestone walls rise over them.

OTHER TOP SITES

HA LONG BAY

HOI AN ANCIENT TOWN

HUE IMPERIAL CITY

SAPA TERRACES

Up ahead, the hikers see a faint light. They walk carefully toward it. Soon they discover a vast, bright space open to the sky. Years ago, the roof of the cave fell in at that spot. Now, towering trees and climbing vines grow there. It is a thick, beautiful jungle. This is Vietnam!

LOCATION

Vietnam is a narrow, S-shaped country. It covers 127,881 miles (331,210 square kilometers) of southeastern Asia. Hanoi, its capital, sits in the north.

Cambodia and Laos curve along Vietnam's western border. To the north rests China. In the northeast, the **Gulf** of Tonkin washes onto Vietnam's shores. The waters of the South China Sea are to the southeast. The Gulf of Thailand forms the country's southwestern border. Thousands of islands, many in Ha Long Bay to the northeast, dot Vietnam's coast.

N
W + E
S

CHINA

HANOI   HAIPHONG

HA LONG
BAY

LAOS

GULF
OF TONKIN

THAILAND

VIETNAM

CAMBODIA

SOUTH
CHINA SEA

HO CHI MINH
CITY

CAN THO

GULF
OF THAILAND

LANDSCAPE AND CLIMATE

Rugged hills and mountains cover most of Vietnam. The country's tallest peak, Fan Si Pan, is in the northwest. It towers at 10,312 feet (3,143 meters). In the shadows below, the Red River winds its way to the Gulf of Tonkin. Along the eastern coastline are narrow bands of lowlands. The forested Truong Son Mountains trail down Vietnam's western border. A protected area of forest called the Green Corridor stands in central Vietnam. Farther south, the Mekong River cuts through the country's **plains**.

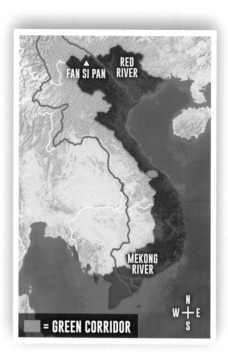

= GREEN CORRIDOR

FAN SI PAN
SAPA

BACH MA NATIONAL PARK
THE GREEN CORRIDOR

HANOI

Average seasonal highs and lows

JANUARY
HIGH: 66 °F (19 °C)
LOW: 58 °F (14 °C)

APRIL
HIGH: 80 °F (27 °C)
LOW: 71 °F (22 °C)

JULY
HIGH: 90 °F (32 °C)
LOW: 80 °F (27 °C)

OCTOBER
HIGH: 82 °F (28 °C)
LOW: 73 °F (23 °C)

°F = degrees Fahrenheit
°C = degrees Celsius

MAGICAL CORRIDOR

The Green Corridor shelters many rare animals. Saolas were discovered there in 1992. These antelope-like animals are nicknamed "Asian unicorns!"

Vietnam experiences two main seasons. Between May and October, **monsoons** bring hot temperatures and heavy rain. November through April is warm and relatively dry. Still, light rain often falls.

WILDLIFE

Vietnam's forests host many different animals. Clouded leopards stalk gibbons and slow lorises high in the trees. Binturongs use their strong tails to climb from branch to branch. On the ground below, rhesus monkeys search for roots and insects. Long claws help Malayan sun bears tear into tree trunks in search of insects.

Hoopoes, great hornbills, and bee-eaters are among the hundreds of bird species found in Vietnam. Yellow-lipped sea kraits slither around Vietnam's southern waters. Dugongs graze in shallow seagrass beds along the coasts.

SLOW LORIS

BINTURONG

YELLOW-LIPPED SEA KRAIT

DUGONG

HOOPOE

10

CLOUDED
LEOPARD

CLOUDED LEOPARD

Life Span: 12-15 years
Red List Status: vulnerable

clouded leopard range = ▪

LEAST CONCERN	NEAR THREATENED	VULNERABLE	ENDANGERED	CRITICALLY ENDANGERED	EXTINCT IN THE WILD	EXTINCT

More than 96 million people live in Vietnam. They make up about 50 **ethnic** groups. Most Vietnamese are Kinh. Their **ancestors** were **native** to the country. Thai, Tay, and Khmer are some of Vietnam's smaller groups. Vietnamese is the country's official language. Each ethnic group also has its own language or **dialect**.

About four out of five Vietnamese are not religious. Of the religions practiced, Buddhism is the most common. A small number of Vietnamese are Christians. In the highlands, folk religions are more common.

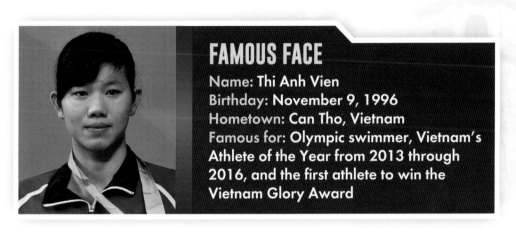

FAMOUS FACE

Name: **Thi Anh Vien**
Birthday: **November 9, 1996**
Hometown: **Can Tho, Vietnam**
Famous for: **Olympic swimmer, Vietnam's Athlete of the Year from 2013 through 2016, and the first athlete to win the Vietnam Glory Award**

SPEAK VIETNAMESE

ENGLISH	VIETNAMESE	HOW TO SAY IT
hello	xin chào	sin JOW
goodbye	tam biêt	TAHM by-ET
please	làm o'n	LAHM uhn
thank you	càm o'n	KAHM uhn
yes	vâng	VUHNG
no	không	KOWM

SOC TRANG

COMMUNITIES

About two out of three Vietnamese live in the countryside. Many **rural** villages are found in the valleys along the Mekong River and Red River. These homes may be built of wood or brick. Inside, one large room often serves as both the living and sleeping space for the entire family.

FLOATING FAMILIES

Rafts and boats anchor in northeastern Vietnam's Ha Long Bay. They form small floating villages. These communities may be more than 15 miles (24 kilometers) from land!

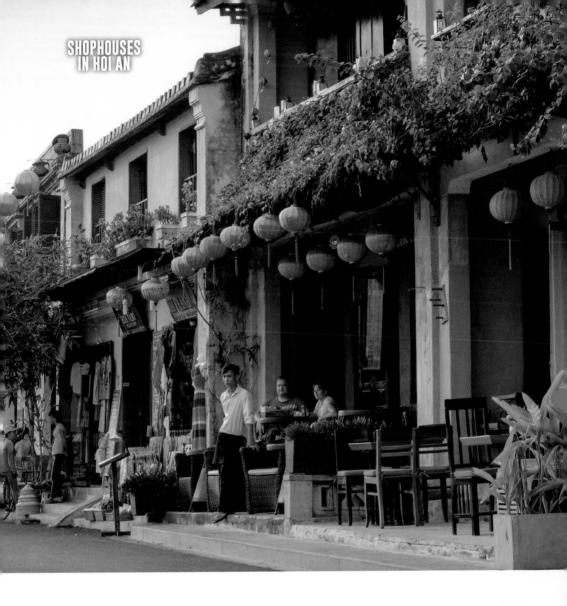

Urban families usually live in small apartments. Shophouses are also common. In each shophouse, a family runs a shop on the building's ground level and lives on the upper floors. Both in the city and the country, multiple generations tend to share a home. **Traditionally**, children are expected to care for their elderly parents. But **nuclear families** are becoming more common.

CUSTOMS

HANDS OFF

In Vietnam, it is rude to touch the top of a person's head. The head is considered very sacred!

AO DAI

Vietnam's citizens have a strong love for their country and its independence. They greatly value teamwork and respect. To greet others, they may shake hands or offer a slight bow.

Lightweight clothing keep Vietnamese cool in the **tropical** heat. In the countryside, cone-shaped hats called *non la* protect workers from the sun. In cities, Western-style clothing for men and women is more common. However, women may wear loose-fitting pants under traditional *ao dai* **tunics**.

NON LA

Vietnamese take education very seriously. Children must attend nine years of school, beginning at age 6. Many continue on to high school. School days are only four hours long, but classes are held six days a week. Many students also take private lessons. After graduating, some students receive job training. Others attend university.

Almost half of Vietnam's workers are farmers. Rice is a key crop and a major **export**. Farmers also grow sugarcane, cashews, and coffee. Along the coasts, fishers catch fresh seafood. Other Vietnamese work in factories to produce clothing, electronics, and cars. The country's millions of yearly visitors create **service jobs** for many of Vietnam's citizens.

CLOTHING FACTORY

SAPA

FARMING THE HILLS

Vietnam's rice farmers have found a way to farm the country's hilly land. They carve step-like levels called terraces into the slopes!

SOCCER

Soccer is the most popular sport in Vietnam. Passionate fans wear jerseys and wave flags to cheer on the national team. The country's lakes and rivers are perfect for water sports like swimming, water skiing, and boat racing. Vietnamese also practice traditional **martial arts** such as *vovinam* or *dau vat*. Vovinam fighters duel with their hands, bamboo sticks, and other weapons. In dau vat matches, fighters wrestle one another in short, fast rounds.

SON MAI

Son mai artists paint layers of colorful sap, called lacquer, onto pieces of black plywood. They sand and polish the lacquer to a bright finish. These beautiful paintings may take months to complete!

Many Vietnamese enjoy watching water puppet shows. The performances often take place on ponds or stages covered in waist-deep water. From behind a screen, performers control wooden puppets. Meanwhile, a live band plays folk music.

PUPPET SHOW

DRAGON PUPPET

Water puppets act out scenes from everyday village life and traditional folktales. Fire-breathing dragons are common characters!

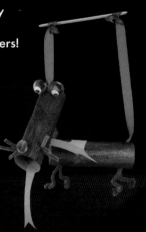

What You Need:
- 2 toilet paper tubes, painted
- tacky glue
- 3 pom-poms
- scissors
- colorful construction paper
- colorful ribbon
- popsicle stick
- googly eyes
- other decorations (optional)

Instructions:
1. Glue two pom-poms on the rim of one tube. These are the eyes. Glue the third pom-pom on the rim across from them. This is the nose.

2. Cut a long strip of paper. Glue it to the inside rim of the tube opposite the nose. This is the tongue.

3. Make two holes in the second tube, one at each end. Make a hole in the first tube between the eyes. Make another hole in the bottom of the tube, directly below the first.

4. Cut a 24-inch (61-centimeter) strip of ribbon. Tie it to one side of the popsicle stick. Thread the ribbon down through the holes of the second tube. Thread it up through the holes of the first tube. Secure it to the other side of the popsicle stick.

5. Add googly eyes, pipe cleaner whiskers, or other decorations if you'd like. Then perform a show of your own! Use the popsicle stick to control your dragon's movements.

Dinner is the most important meal in Vietnam. Families come together to share food and discuss the day. Different dishes, such as stir-fried fish and vegetables, sit at the center of the table. Using chopsticks, people take small servings from each dish and add them to their own rice bowls. Rice is a **staple** at meals.

A soup called *pho* is Vietnam's national dish. It is made up of broth, rice noodles, fresh herbs, and meat. *Goi cuon*, or spring rolls, are another favorite. These stuffed rice paper wrappers often feature pork, shrimp, rice noodles, and greens. *Nuoc mam*, or fish sauce, is a popular **condiment** found on many Vietnamese tables.

PHO

NUOC MAM

GOI CUON (SPRING ROLLS) RECIPE

Ingredients:
1 package rice paper wrappers
warm water
1 cucumber, sliced into thin strips
1 carrot, sliced into thin strips
1 head of leaf lettuce, thinly chopped
1 bunch of mint
1 bunch of chives
1 package vermicelli rice noodles, cooked
1/2 pound medium-sized shrimp, boiled
fish sauce, for dipping

Steps:
1. Dip a piece of rice paper into a bowl of warm water for a few seconds. This makes the paper easier to work with. Lay the rice paper out flat.

2. Take a little of each vegetable and herb. Place them along one side of the paper. Put some of the noodles on top. Add shrimp. Do not use too many ingredients, or you will not be able to roll it all up!

3. Begin to roll up the paper from the side with the ingredients. Tuck in the ends as you roll. The roll should be snug but not too tight.

4. Repeat until you run out of ingredients.

5. Eat immediately. Dip them in fish sauce for extra flavor!

TET NGUYEN DAN

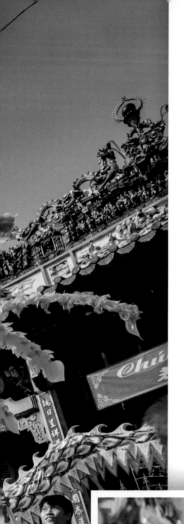

Tet Nguyen Dan, the lunar new year, is Vietnam's major holiday. It falls in late January or early February. This seven-day festival brings family gatherings, feasts, and gift giving. Crowds gather to watch the traditional dragon and lion dances.

In the spring, Buddhist Vietnamese travel north for the Huong **Pagoda** Festival. They visit this mountain pagoda to worship Buddha and pray for their families. On September 2, Vietnam celebrates National Day. It honors the day Vietnam became an independent country. Waving flags, parades, and fireworks help the Vietnamese celebrate the land they love.

MOON FESTIVAL

The harvest moon brings *Tet Trung Thu*, or the Mid-Autumn Festival. It is a time of celebration for children. They wear bright masks, wave star-shaped lanterns, and snack on sweet mooncakes.

25

TIMELINE

939 CE
Vietnam gains independence from China

207 BCE
A Chinese general establishes the Nam Viet kingdom in parts of today's Vietnam, starting Chinese rule

1945
Leader Ho Chi Minh declares Vietnam's independence from France

1860s
Vietnam becomes a colony of France

ABOUT 800 BCE
The Dong Son community develops near the Red River valley

1976
North Vietnam and South Vietnam join to form the Socialist Republic of Vietnam

1954
The Geneva Accords officially divide Vietnam into two zones, South Vietnam and communist North Vietnam

1992
Vietnam adopts a new constitution

TRAN DAI QUANG

1957
Start of the Vietnam War, which lasts until South Vietnam's defeat in 1975

2016
Vietnam elects Tran Dai Quang as president and Nguyen Xuan Phuc as prime minister

VIETNAM FACTS

Official Name: Socialist Republic of Vietnam

Flag of Vietnam: Vietnam's flag features a yellow, five-pointed star in the center of a red background. The red represents the blood spilled in revolution. The star is a symbol for communism. Its points stand for the groups of people who together make communism possible. Vietnam adopted this flag in 1945.

Area: 127,881 square miles
(331,210 square kilometers)

Capital City: Hanoi

Important Cities: Ho Chi Minh City, Can Tho, Haiphong

Population:
96,160,163 (July 2017)

WHERE PEOPLE LIVE

COUNTRYSIDE
65.1%

CITY
34.9%

JOBS

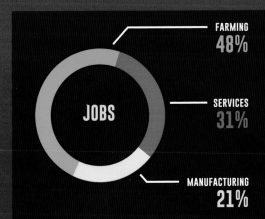

FARMING
48%

SERVICES
31%

MANUFACTURING
21%

Main Exports:

oil

electronics

clothing

rice

seafood

machinery

National Holiday:
Independence Day (September 2)

Main Language:
Vietnamese

Form of Government:
communism

Title for Country Leaders:
president, prime minister

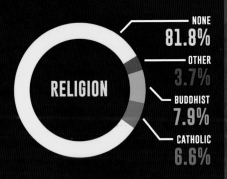

RELIGION

NONE
81.8%

OTHER
3.7%

BUDDHIST
7.9%

CATHOLIC
6.6%

Unit of Money:
dong

GLOSSARY

ancestors—relatives who lived long ago

condiment—a seasoning for food

dialect—a local way of speaking a particular language

ethnic—related to a group of people who share customs and an identity

export—a product sold by one country to another

gulf—part of an ocean or sea that extends into land

martial arts—styles and techniques of fighting and self-defense that are practiced as sport

monsoons—winds that shift direction each season; monsoons bring heavy rain.

native—originally from the area or related to a group of people that began in the area

nuclear families—families that include only the parents and children

pagoda—a temple made of multiple stories

plains—large areas of flat land

rugged—rough and uneven

rural—related to the countryside

service jobs—jobs that perform tasks for people or businesses

staple—a widely used food or other item

traditionally—in keeping with the customs, ideas, or beliefs handed down from one generation to the next

tropical—relating to the tropics; the tropics is a hot, rainy region near the equator.

tunics—long, tight-fitting shirts or jackets with high collars

urban—related to cities and city life

TO LEARN MORE

AT THE LIBRARY

Rau, Dana Meachen. *It's Cool to Learn About Countries: Vietnam.* Ann Arbor, Mich.: Cherry Lake Publishing, 2012.

Tran, Phuoc Thi Minh. *Vietnamese Children's Favorite Stories.* Tokyo, Japan: Tuttle Publishing, 2015.

Yasuda, Anita. *Vietnam.* New York, N.Y.: AV2 by Weigl, 2017.

ON THE WEB

Learning more about Vietnam is as easy as 1, 2, 3.

1. Go to www.factsurfer.com.

2. Enter "Vietnam" into the search box.

3. Click the "Surf" button and you will see a list of related web sites.

With factsurfer.com, finding more information is just a click away.

INDEX

The images in this book are reproduced through the courtesy of: Gerhard Zwerger-Schoner/ ImageBroker, front cover; Vietnam Stock Images, pp. 4-5; Efired, pp. 5 (top), 26 (top); Michal Jastrzebski, p. 5 (middle top); Oleskaus, p. 5 (middle bottom); Blue Planet Studio, p. 5 (bottom); Brittany McIntosh, pp. 6-7, 8 (inset); May Chanikran, p. 8; Thoai, pp. 9 (inset), 13 (bottom); Hryorii Patlakha, p. 9; Hoang Mai Thach, p. 10 (top); Andrey Tau, p. 10 (middle top); Ibeirodos Santos, p. 10 (middle bottom); Fidel, p. 10 (bottom left); Laura Dinraths, p. 10 (bottom right); Sarah Cheriton-Jones, pp. 10-11; John Bill, p. 12; Philippe Lopez/ Getty Images, p. 13 (top); RM Numes, p. 14; Alex Robinson/ Getty Images, p. 15; Jimmy Tran, pp. 16, 19 (top); Sirisak Baokaew, pp. 17, 19 (bottom); Inga Spence/ Alamy, p. 18; Moo in Black, p. 20 (top); Jose More/ Alamy, p. 20 (bottom); Nadezda Zavitaeva, p. 21 (top); Tami Peterson, p. 21 (bottom); Xuan Huongho, pp. 22, 23 (bottom); LA the Crocodile, p. 23 (top); Qragon, p. 23 (middle); www.jethuynh.com/ Getty Images, pp. 24-25; Yulia Aksa, p. 24 (inset); DEA Picture Library/ Getty Images, p. 26 (bottom); Presidential Communications Operations Office, p. 27; Alan Bauman, p. 28 (flag); Miroslav, p. 29 (currency); Andrey Lobachev, p. 29 (coin).